ANASTASIA'S ALBUM

ISBN 0-590-26004-9

12 11 10 9 8 7 6 5 4 3 2 1   7 8 9/9 0 1 2/0

Printed in the U.S.A.   08
First Scholastic printing, October 1997

Previous page: *A framed portrait of Anastasia, aged eight.*
Opposite: *One of the splendid rooms of the Catherine Palace at Tsarskoe Selo today and a 1909 portrait of Anastasia in formal dress.*

ANASTASIA'S
ALBUM *by* HUGH BREWSTER

SCHOLASTIC INC.
New York Toronto London Auckland Sydney

The gates to one of the two palaces at Tsarskoe Selo, the "tsar's village," where Anastasia lived with her family.

Prologue

Behind the palace gates once lived a girl named Anastasia. Her father was Tsar Nicholas II, who ruled over the vast Russian empire. Even though Anastasia and her sisters and brother lived in a palace with hundreds of servants, they enjoyed playing games and doing the things other families do. Anastasia loved to take photographs of their activities and then paste them into albums. Sometimes she would decorate the album pages and add color to the photographs. Thanks to Anastasia's albums and letters, we can now step behind the palace gates and see what life was really like for the last ruling family of Russia.

> **"** *I took this picture while looking in the mirror and it was hard, because my hands were shaking.* **"**
>
> —From a letter to her father

Chapter One
Babyhood

1901-1904

66 *Around 3 A.M. Alexandra started having strong pain.... Exactly at 6 A.M. my daughter was born—Anastasia.* 99

—From the diary of
Tsar Nicholas II, June 18, 1901

It was spring 1901. Even in the chilly Russian capital of St. Petersburg, the ice had melted on the canals, and the lilacs were in bloom. On days when the wind blew away the fog, the city's magnificent cathedrals and mansions glistened along the broad avenues and canals. All over Russia, people welcomed the end of another long winter.

There were many reasons to be hopeful this year. The entire country awaited the birth of a baby. Tsar Nicholas II and his wife, Alexandra, were expecting their fourth child. The tsar and tsarina already had three beautiful, rosy-cheeked daughters, but in Russia only males could rule. So this time Nicholas and Alexandra wished for a boy, who would be heir to the throne.

On Wednesday, June 18, a healthy child was born in the imperial family's summer villa on the seashore north of St. Petersburg. When Tsar Nicholas heard that the child was a girl, he went for a long walk by himself. Then he put a smile on his face and went in to kiss his wife and newborn baby. Her name was Anastasia, and she was the newest of the Romanovs—the family that ruled the biggest country on earth.

*Baby Anastasia with her mother (opposite).
Anastasia was born in the family's summer house, or dacha, at Peterhof
(right) on the Baltic Sea, not far from the Great Palace (above). This
palace had been built two hundred years before by Tsar Peter the Great.*

Two weeks later the tsar's fourth daughter was christened. Her official title was "Her Imperial Highness the Grand Duchess Anastasia Nicholaievna." (The tsar's daughters were called grand duchesses to show that they were even grander than mere princesses.) After the christening, the family had a formal photograph taken. As much as they had longed for a son, Nicholas and Alexandra were grateful to have yet another beautiful, healthy baby girl.

Anastasia and her family spent part of each winter at the magnificent Winter Palace in St. Petersburg. The enormous building was spread over three city blocks and had high ceilings, marble columns, wide staircases, and giant chandeliers. Huge mirrors lined the corridors.

For the Russian aristocracy and upper classes, life during the winter in St. Petersburg was one endless party. There was a steady stream of fancy teas, luncheons, and dinners. There were concerts, operas, and ballets to attend.

This family photograph was taken in honor of Anastasia's christening. Alexandra was wearing black because her grandmother, Queen Victoria of England, had recently died. (Above) The imperial family's baby crib.

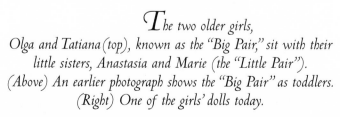

*T*he two older girls,
Olga and Tatiana (top), known as the "Big Pair," sit with their
little sisters, Anastasia and Marie (the "Little Pair").
(Above) An earlier photograph shows the "Big Pair" as toddlers.
(Right) One of the girls' dolls today.

Most fabulous of all were the imperial grand balls. On the evenings when they were held, a torch-lit procession of carriages or sleighs would pull up in front of the Winter Palace. The men wore dashing uniforms and the women dressed in their finest satin gowns, covered with diamonds, emeralds, and sapphires. Guests ate a lavish supper at midnight and danced until dawn.

The tsar and his wife were expected to be at the center of every great occasion. But Nicholas and Alexandra did not enjoy the social whirl very much. They would leave the court balls as early as possible, nodding politely to the courtiers and servants, who stood in rows, bowing.

Guests pose at the Winter Palace during an elaborate costume ball in 1903. This ostrich fan was part of the costume of Anastasia's Aunt Xenia. (Left) Alexandra, dressed for a formal court occasion. (Opposite) Three-year-old Anastasia (at right) with her sisters.

Once inside their private apartments, they sighed with relief as they took off their formal clothes. Then they would tiptoe into the nursery to see their four sleeping daughters. Tenderly they would kiss and tuck in each one—clever Olga, delicate Tatiana, chubby little Marie, and finally the baby, golden-haired Anastasia. Once their official duties were over, the tsar and his wife liked nothing better than to board the blue imperial train with their young family and escape to the Alexander Palace at

Tsarskoe Selo, or the "tsar's village." Here, outside high iron railings, Cossack horsemen armed with sabers guarded both the Alexander Palace and the immense blue-and-white Catherine Palace. The surrounding park included beautiful lawns and gardens, fountains and bridges, pavilions and statues. In a small lake behind the palace there was a children's island, where Anastasia and her sisters had their own playhouse.

By the time she was three, Anastasia was a blue-eyed whirlwind, running and playing on the palace grounds. She already had a mind and personality of her own. Noisy and fearless, she rarely cried, even when she hurt herself. She was the baby of the family, adored by her parents and sisters.

But Russia still had no heir to the throne. During the summer of 1904, as Alexandra prepared to give birth to her fifth child, everyone in the household wanted only one thing: a boy who would carry on the mighty Romanov dynasty. On August 12, Alexandra felt pains during lunch and went upstairs to her bedroom. That evening Nicholas wrote in his diary, "A great, never-to-be-forgotten day.... At 1:15 this afternoon Alexandra gave birth to a son, whom in prayer we have called Alexei."

In cities and towns throughout the vast land, church bells rang, cannons roared, and there was great rejoicing. But for many Russians the birth of an heir to the throne was not a reason to celebrate. They were becoming impatient with the rule of the tsar

Every Easter, Tsar Nicholas presented his wife with a fabulous Easter egg. Created by the court jeweler, Fabergé, each egg had a tiny surprise inside it. This egg is made of gold, rubies, and diamonds and is decorated with lilies of the valley made of pearls. The surprise is three tiny jeweled portraits of Nicholas and his daughters Olga and Tatiana. (Opposite top) The family with the newborn Alexei. (Opposite right) The tsar with his baby son.

and wanted Russia to have a more democratic government. Eighty percent of Russia's people were peasant farmers who lived in poverty. Many of them worked in the fields of wealthy landowners. In the cities factory workers received very low wages and lived in miserable slums. Changes were desperately needed in Russia. But Nicholas said that those who wanted reform were "senseless dreamers." Like all the tsars before him, he believed that God had given him the right to reign. He felt that with the simple goodwill and faith of the people, the Romanovs would continue to rule Russia as they had for almost three hundred years. He was to be proven wrong.

Anastasia stands beside two-year-old Alexei, who holds a box camera (left). (Bottom left) Alexandra has taken the camera and tries to pose her children for a picture. (Below) The family on board the royal yacht, the Standart. The sailor Derevenko (opposite left) looked after Alexei for many years. (Opposite right) Alexei on the Standart, age four. (Opposite bottom) Alexei's toy drum and cannon today.

How beautiful he was, how healthy, how normal, with his golden hair, his shining blue eyes... —From the memoirs of Anna Vyrubova, family friend

When baby Alexei began to crawl, dark bruises appeared on his legs and arms. His mother noticed them and became frightened. Soon she learned the terrible truth. Her son was a hemophiliac. His blood did not clot properly, and any bump or fall could cause serious internal bleeding. Two sailors from the royal yacht were assigned to watch and protect him at all times.

The Alexander Palace today (above). The family's private quarters were in the wing on the right-hand side. (Left) Two of the palace's formal rooms as they once looked.

Chapter Two

A Life Apart

1905–1910

Anastasia was only three when her brother was born and too young to understand what hemophilia was. But the whole family knew that Alexei's ailment was a secret. They had decided that the Russian people must not know that the heir to the throne would never be healthy. From 1905 on, the family spent more and more time behind the gates of Tsarskoe Selo. This was also for their own protection.

The year after Alexei was born, strikes, demonstrations, and riots against the absolute rule of the tsar broke out all across Russia. When some protesters marched peacefully on the Winter Palace, the tsar's soldiers fired on them and hundreds were killed. To stop the protests against his rule, Nicholas had to give up some of his powers to an elected parliament called the *Duma*.

Alexandra decorated the family's private rooms with brightly colored wallpaper and fabric, as shown in this sketch (above), which she drew for her daughters. The bold patterns that she liked can be seen in a 1906 photograph (right) of Olga (at right) and Tatiana.

But Anastasia and her sisters knew little about politics. And they loved living at Tsarskoe Selo. Although the Alexander Palace there had more than one hundred elegant rooms, the family's private quarters were simply and comfortably furnished. Anastasia's mother had freshly cut flowers delivered throughout the year, and their fragrance filled every room. The Romanovs had a warm and intimate family life, but in many ways it was strict, too. The four grand duchesses slept on hard camp cots with no pillows, just as their father had done when he was a boy. Every morning they made their own beds and had a cold bath in a tub made of solid silver.

In those days girls of the upper classes were expected to learn only the skills that would help them pass the time once they were married—how to play the piano, sketch flowers, and do a little needlework. But the girls' mother demanded more. The children studied four languages—Russian, English, French, and German. Alexandra carefully chose books for them to read and supervised their music lessons. And although the grand duchesses had private teachers, the tsarina spent much time in the palace schoolroom herself, keeping a close eye on her daughters' lessons.

Still, the little girls had plenty of playtime. Their nursery was filled with miniature versions of grown-up furniture and decorated with flowers and ferns. Nurses, one for each child, made sure their hair was brushed and their matching dresses were always fresh. The grand duchesses had dozens of fine porcelain dolls, many of them presents from their mother's English relatives or visiting royalty. Inside the palace, they played with

Anastasia shares a secret with her young brother (above). Her three older sisters (right) pose with their bicycles at Peterhof.

*The four sisters are dressed to go swimming at Peterhof in 1905.
Four-year-old Anastasia is on the far right. Next to her is Marie, then Tatiana and then the oldest, Olga, aged nine.*

their doll carriages, music boxes, and toy animals. On the palace grounds, they rode tricycles and bicycles.

The girls would visit their mother every morning in her boudoir, where all the furnishings, even the curtains and carpets, were mauve. It was a cozy room next to her bedroom, cluttered with books and photographs and cushions, and filled with the scent of the pink and purple flowers that she loved. Alexandra kept a big basket full of toys there, and the girls would climb up on the bed with her, or sit on the carpet and play while she embroidered or knitted.

Every afternoon the whole family gathered for tea. The girls wore fresh ribbons in their hair and clean white dresses with

*T*he girls liked to draw
pictures of their mother (above) dressed in formal clothes (right) for
special occasions. (Opposite top) A beautiful picture of (from left) Olga, Tatiana, Marie,
and Anastasia, taken in 1906. (Opposite bottom) Anastasia sits next to Alexandra in the
mauve boudoir. Marie (at right) and Tatiana are in front.

colored sashes. They would wait impatiently for their father's arrival. He would eat one piece of bread and butter and drink two glasses of tea while he read his newspapers. Anastasia, Marie, and Alexei would play with their toys. The two older girls, Olga and Tatiana, worked on their knitting.

Tea was one of the few times during the day that the children saw their father, but they understood why. After all, he was probably one of the most important people in the world. Government ministers, church leaders, and grand dukes bowed before him. Even their mother bowed to him in public. Whenever he went out, the entire household stood respectfully by the windows of the palace until he had walked to his carriage or car and been driven off.

To the outside world Tsar Nicholas was the ruler of millions, but to his children he was simply their beloved father. He was handsome and gentle, and he never raised his voice. The girls spent hours making drawings and paintings for him and writing little notes, carefully trying to do their best work to please him.

He was just their papa, and they were a family like any other.

> **She was the imp of the whole house and the glummest faces would always brighten in her presence, for it was impossible to resist her jokes and nonsense.**
>
> —From the memoirs of Pierre Gilliard, the children's French tutor

Anastasia's family nickname was *Shvibzik*, which means "imp" in Russian. Years later, her father's sister Grand Duchess Olga recalled Anastasia's hilarious imitations of some of the pompous people who visited the palace. "That is how I remember her," Olga wrote, "brimming with life and mischief and laughing so often."

Anastasia making faces for the camera (right). In a more serious mood, she practices her knitting (opposite) on a piano stool in her mother's boudoir. Anastasia also loved to paint and draw. In 1914, she painted the picture shown above and sent it in a letter to her father, perhaps to remind him of her as a little girl.

"*Dear, sweet Mama,*

I am writing you such a long letter before dinner on purpose. I want to talk to you on the telephone after dinner, may I? I really want to.... I hope that when we come you will be already feeling better. Mama, I won't make jokes with the officers. I will try to be gay and not show that I was crying. Tell me when are you going to have dinner? Sleep well and be healthy, take care of yourself. Loving you with all my heart and soul."

—A note from Anastasia to her ill mother

Alexandra was often unwell after Alexei was born. She worried constantly about her son's health and suffered greatly when he had one of his attacks of severe bleeding. The strain took its toll on her own health and sometimes she would stay in her mauve boudoir for days at a time. The only person who was able to bring comfort to both the tsarina and her son was a bearded monk named Rasputin. When Rasputin prayed or laid his hands on Alexei, his bleeding would miraculously stop. To Alexandra, Rasputin was a gift from God. But many important people thought he was a fraud. They also resented the fact that a poor peasant had become a person of such importance to the imperial family.

A decorated album page (opposite) shows Alexandra in her boudoir (top left and bottom center) and on the balcony outside it with her children (bottom left). Anastasia stands outside the palace with Alexei (top center), slides on the frozen lake (top right), and skates with her sister Olga (bottom right).

❝ *Oh, if you knew how hard Mama's illness is for us to bear.* ❞

—From a letter by Tatiana to the monk Rasputin

66 *Everything here is covered with snow and everyone is going
sleighing and skiing and even skating on ice.* 99

—From a letter to her father

THE SCHOOLROOM

Anastasia found schoolwork boring. Her French tutor, Pierre Gilliard, described her as "a lazy pupil." Her English teacher, Charles Gibbes, remembered her trying to bribe him with flowers so he would raise her poor marks. When he refused, she gave them to the Russian teacher, Peter Petrov, who was a favorite of hers.

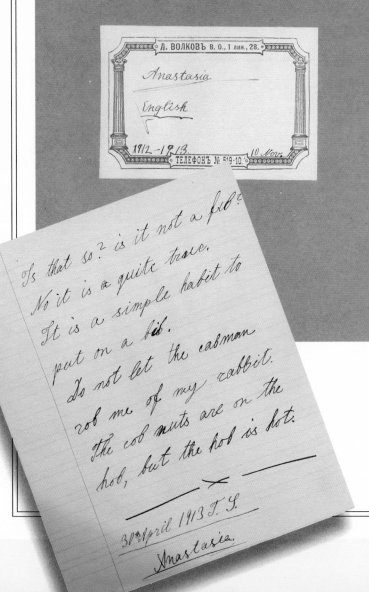

Is that so.? is it not a fib?
No it is a quite true.
It is a simple habit to
put on a bib.
Do not let the cabman
rob me of my rabbit.
The cob nuts are on the
hob, but the hob is hot.

30th April 1913 J. S.

Anastasia.

66 *Now I have to do an arithmetical problem and of course it doesn't want to solve, such pig and filth!* 99

—From a letter to Peter Petrov

Anastasia in the schoolroom with her English teacher, Charles Gibbes (opposite top). A page from her English workbook is at opposite left. All the girls were very fond of the Russian teacher, Peter Petrov, shown in a sketch by Tatiana (opposite right). Unlike Anastasia, Marie (left) enjoyed schoolwork. The children's French tutor, Pierre Gilliard (below), stayed with the family for many years.

66 *What we did yesterday to M. Gilliard—just terrible. We were pushing him with our fists and in any other way, he had it from us!* 99

—From a letter to her father

66 *Marie and I spend every evening with Aunt Olga and we paint a lot... Aunt Olga is so dear, kind, and cheerful, you must be envying me. There are a lot of roses here and other flowers too. I painted with oils and it came out very nicely.* 99

—From a letter to Peter Petrov from Livadia

*A*nastasia's love of painting
and drawing was encouraged by her godmother, Aunt Olga, who was a skilled
artist. Here, at age eleven, she concentrates on a painting in the schoolroom
of her family's summer palace at Livadia. A flower drawing from one of
her sketchbooks is shown at left.

Chapter Three

Imperial Retreats

1911–1914

" *Our rooms here are very large and clean and white and we have real fruit and grapes growing here.... I am so happy that we don't have those horrid lessons. In the evening we all sit together, four of us, the gramophone plays, we listen to it and play together.... I didn't write to you because Alexei came for me and said that I should be going swimming. Papa has now been swimming for a few days, and I am going today for the first time.... I don't miss Tsarskoe Selo at all, because I can't even tell you how bored I am there.* "

—From a letter to Peter Petrov in 1911

LIVADIA

Anastasia and her family especially loved their visits to the palace of Livadia. Every March, when it was still cold in St. Petersburg, they would board the imperial train for the long journey south to the Black Sea. There, flowers would already be blooming in the palace's large gardens. Days at Livadia were filled with hikes, swimming, tennis, and excursions to gather wild berries and mushrooms. In 1911, when Anastasia was ten, a beautiful white marble palace was built there to replace a gloomy old wooden one.

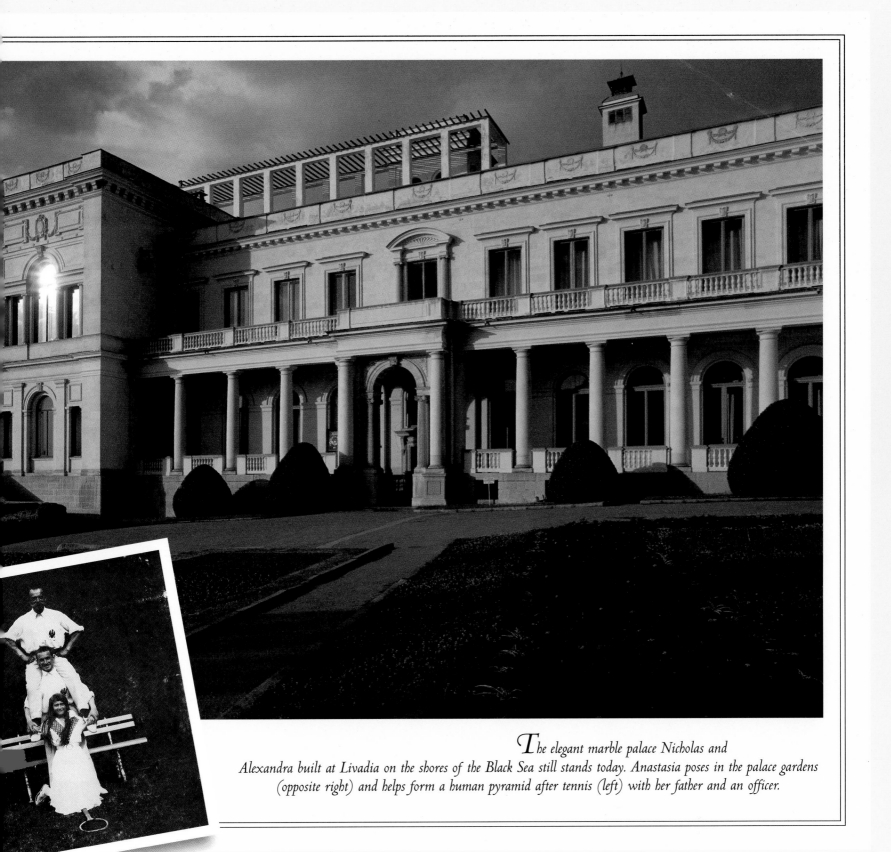

The elegant marble palace Nicholas and Alexandra built at Livadia on the shores of the Black Sea still stands today. Anastasia poses in the palace gardens (opposite right) and helps form a human pyramid after tennis (left) with her father and an officer.

" *Life at Livadia was simple and informal. We walked, rode, bathed in the sea, and generally led a healthful country life, such as the tsar enjoyed to the utmost.* "

—From the memoirs of Anna Vyrubova

Anastasia sits on Livadia's pebbled beach (top left) while (top right) Aunt Olga (at left), Tatiana, and the tsar play in the waves. In the hand-colored photograph at left, Anastasia takes a walk with her father and two of her older sisters. The album page at right shows adventures on a hike to a mountain hunting lodge in May 1913.

Визит.

р. Альма.

козьмо-демьянск.

PETERHOF

For much of the summer, Anastasia and her family lived at their beachfront *dacha*, at Peterhof on the Baltic Sea north of St. Petersburg. From there they would board the royal yacht, the *Standart*, for a July cruise through the islands off the coast of Finland.

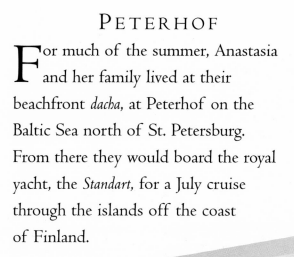

Scenes from the beach at the Peterhof dacha, summer of 1915. (Above) Anastasia's oldest sister Olga (at right) sits on the sand with a friend. The woman with the white dress and crutch (in photos opposite) is the family's friend, Anna Vyrubova, who had been injured in a train crash.

THE STANDART

All year Anastasia looked forward to the family's summer cruise on the *Standart*. It was the most elegant royal yacht in the world and included staterooms for the family, a chapel, and quarters for the servants, the crew, and a platoon of soldiers. For Anastasia and her sisters, the yacht's handsome young officers were welcome company.

> Everyone says I got a lot of suntan. I terribly want to dance and wait for an hour to come when I will dance with the officers. They all love to dance. We will dance on Marie's holiday and every Sunday when my Aunt Olga wants it. I will be writing then very little because I will be all hers and she will be playing all the time.

—From a letter to Peter Petrov

*With camera in hand, Anastasia poses on the Standart
with her sisters in the summer of 1911. (Opposite right) Dancing on the yacht, July 1912. (Opposite left) In a hat
and scarf on a winter cruise to the Black Sea, 1913.*

*A*nastasia painted flowers around
these scenes from the Standart *in her photo album. The page above shows her mother
dressed to greet visitors. At right Alexandra prepares to use her camera and
(far right) poses with her husband and children. In the summer of 1912
(opposite top), Anastasia stands on deck with a sailor and (opposite bottom) sits
belowdecks in her father's study. Marie is in the background.*

"Marie and I recited our French dialogues, everybody liked it very much. Today I went swimming after tennis.... We had cinematograph twice. We are so comfortable here on the yacht."

—From a letter to Peter Petrov

> ❝ *We take long walks with Papa. One day we walked around the whole island—twelve miles.* ❞
>
> —From a letter to Peter Petrov

THE ISLAND

The *Standart* often anchored off a Finnish island the family had chosen as their own. Each day they would go ashore for hikes, picnics, and tennis.

Activities on the island included: walking on stilts (left); pretending to float in midair on a homemade merry-go-round (above) or balancing on it (opposite top right); relaxing after tennis (opposite top left); spending time with her father (opposite bottom right) or swinging (opposite bottom left).

" *Yesterday Marie, Aunt Olga and I walked barefoot. It was great. Alexei is healthy but Mama is not feeling well.... We have new officers here, they are a lot of fun.* **"** —From a letter to Peter Petrov

Anastasia and her Aunt Olga wading offshore from their favorite Finnish island (opposite). (Left) Anastasia was obviously very proud of her pink summer hat. (Below) The girls and the officers from the yacht enjoyed the tennis court on the island.

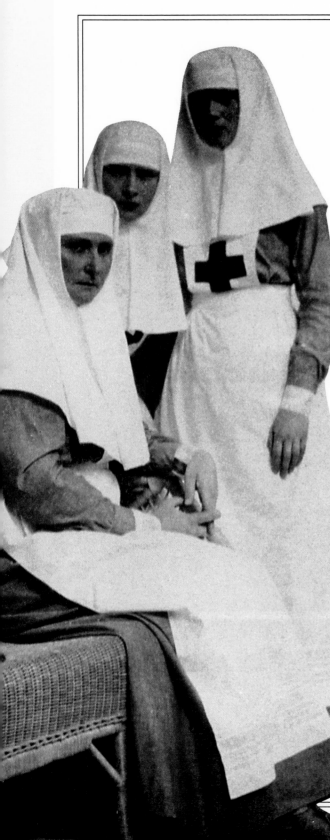

Chapter Four

The War Years

August 1914–March 1917

On August 1, 1914, the tsar arrived home very late for dinner. His face was pale. In a quiet, sad voice he told his wife that Russia was now at war with Germany and Austria.

Alexandra burst into tears and ran from the room. Before her marriage to Nicholas, she had been a German princess. Now her home country was an enemy. The First World War had begun.

Alexandra was determined to do all she could to help Russia win the war. She and her two eldest daughters trained as nurses and worked long hours in military hospitals. Anastasia and Marie were too young to become nurses, but they regularly visited wounded

Alexandra sits next to Tatiana and Olga in their Red Cross nursing uniforms (left). One of their uniforms has been preserved (above). (Opposite) Anastasia visits some of the patients at the war hospital near the palace. Marie stands behind her.

"My dear Papa darling!—I missed my turn to write to you because I didn't have time—we spent a lot of time in our new hospital. In the very first day they brought three officers and twenty privates there, four of them in serious condition. One of them is a sixteen-year-old boy, his wound is also quite serious."

—From a letter to her father

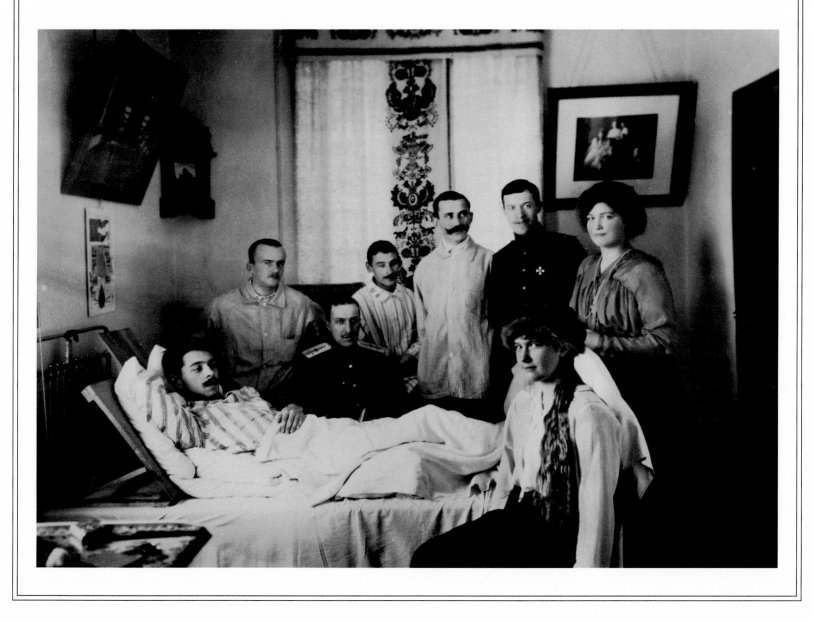

> This afternoon we all went for a ride, went to church and to the hospital, and that's it! And now we have to go eat dinner and then to the hospital again, and this is our life, yes! ""

—From a letter to Peter Petrov

Anastasia (above) perches on the back of a car at Tsarskoe Selo. During the war Alexandra and her daughters (above right) would sometimes visit the tsar at army headquarters in Mogilev. On a family outing in October of 1916, Nicholas and Alexandra rest on a haystack (opposite left) with Marie and Anastasia. (Opposite right) Always the family comic, Anastasia poses with false teeth and crossed eyes in 1915.

soldiers at a small hospital near the Alexander Palace. "I sat today with one of our soldiers and helped him to learn to read," Anastasia wrote to her father. "Two more soldiers died yesterday. We were still with them."

By the beginning of 1915, more than one million Russian soldiers had died in the war. Nicholas decided to take command of the army himself and spent most of his time at the military headquarters, or *stavka*, in western Russia. With her husband away,

Alexandra became more involved in the running of the government. Each day she would write to the tsar, giving her advice and opinions about government ministers and their actions. Many of her ideas were influenced by Rasputin, whom she trusted as a man of God and the savior of her son. Rasputin's power over the tsarina made him many enemies. Wild rumors began that Alexandra and Rasputin were spies for Germany. By the autumn of 1916, more and more people were unhappy with the tsar, the tsarina, and the government. Russian soldiers were dying by the millions in the war. At home their families were going hungry. But Nicholas and Alexandra and their children were not aware of the terrible storm that was approaching.

66 *My Darling Sweet and Dear Papa!! I want to see you very much. I have just finished my arithmetic lesson and it seems to be not bad. Today it is raining and very wet. I am in Tatiana's room. Tatiana and Olga are here. I try my best to get rid of worms, and Olga says I am stinking, but that is untrue. I sat digging my nose with my left hand. Olga wanted to give me a slap, but I escaped from her swinish hand. I hope you have got a good picture of Alexei and you show it to everybody. Tatiana is as stupid as ever. I kiss you a HUNDRED times my dear darling Papa. Olga is adjusting her trousers. When you arrive I shall be meeting you at the station. Be cheerful and healthy. Squeezing fondly your hand and face. Thinking of you. Loving you ever and everywhere from your writing daughter Anastasia.* 99

—A letter to her father

Chapter Five

Revolution

March 1917 - July 1918

An icy wind howled outside the Alexander Palace on the night of March 13, 1917. Anastasia looked out her window at a huge gun that soldiers guarding the palace had set up in the courtyard. "How astonished Papa will be," she whispered. Her father was expected back from the *stavka* early the next morning. In the distance Anastasia could hear shouting and gunfire. Her mother had told her that the soldiers were just doing military exercises. Alexandra did not want to frighten her children with the truth. She knew that strikes and rioting in St. Petersburg had spread and that angry mobs were threatening to attack the palace. She did not yet know that a revolution had started.

Late the next morning the tsar's train had still not arrived. "But the train is *never* late," Anastasia declared. "Oh, if Papa would only come quickly.... I'm beginning to feel ill. What shall I do if I get ill? I can't be useful to Mama." Olga, Tatiana, and Alexei were all in bed with the measles and

The Alexander Palace in winter today (above). (Left) A soldier stands guard over the former tsar in April 1917. Anastasia took this photograph of her father and Tatiana, who had been clearing ice from the canal in the palace grounds.

Anastasia had been running errands for her mother. Now she, too, was coming down with measles. "Please don't let me be ill. Please don't keep me in bed," she kept repeating. "Everything will be all right when Papa comes home."

But it would be over a week before her father returned. And when he did he was no longer the tsar. Members of the *Duma* had formed their own government in St. Petersburg. To prevent further rioting and bloodshed they had asked Nicholas to give up his throne. At the urging of his generals he had agreed. The Romanov family had ruled Russia for over three hundred years. Now Nicholas Romanov was just an ordinary citizen—and a prisoner in his own palace. Soldiers loyal to the new revolutionary government kept the family under constant guard.

But for a while, life in the Alexander Palace went on almost as it had before. Lessons continued in the schoolroom. Nicholas and his children were allowed to take walks on the palace grounds in the afternoon. When spring came they were given permission to dig a vegetable garden. Sometimes crowds would gather at the palace gates to jeer at them as they worked.

Anastasia and her family hoped they would be allowed to live at their beloved Livadia. But instead they learned they were being sent to Siberia. Early on the morning of August 14, the family left the Alexander Palace for the last time. "What shall the future bring to my poor children?" Alexandra wrote to a friend. "My heart breaks thinking of them."

Tatiana and Anastasia (top) enjoy a beautiful day on the grounds of the Alexander Palace in June of 1917. In the background stand some of their guards. Alexei (above) plays with his spaniel, Joy, who went with him to Siberia.

" We finished our kitchen garden some time ago and it is now in splendid condition. We have every imaginable kind of vegetable and five hundred cabbages. "

—From the diary of Pierre Gilliard, June 19, 1917

Creating the vegetable garden (from top): Tatiana helping to carry sod; Tatiana and Anastasia wheeling a water barrel; Alexandra—in a wheelchair because of her poor health—embroiders while watching the activity; the four girls resting from their work (Anastasia is second from right).

66 *As the grand duchesses were losing their hair as a result of their measles, their heads have been shaved. When they go out in the park they wear scarves arranged so as to conceal the fact. Just as I was going to take their photograph, they all suddenly removed their headdress. I protested, but they insisted, much amused at the idea, and looking forward to seeing the indignant surprise of their parents. Their good spirits reappear from time to time in spite of everything.* 99

—From the diary of Pierre Gilliard, June 22, 1917

" *My Dear Friend,* [written in English on the train to Siberia with Anastasia's own spelling] *I will describe to you who [how] we traveled. We started in the morning and when we got into the train I went to sleap, so did all of us. We were very tierd because we did not sleap the whole night. The first day was hot and very dusty. At the stations we had to shut our window curtanse that nobody should see us. Once in the evening I was looking out we stoped near a little house, but there was no station so we could look out. A little boy came to my window and asked: "Uncle, please give me, if you have got, a newspaper." I said: "I am not an uncle but an anty and have no newspaper." At the first moment I could not understand why did he call me "Uncle" but then I remembered that my hear is cut and I and the soldiers (which where standing next to me) laught very much.*
On the way many funy things had hapend, and if I shall have time I shall write to you our travell farther on. Good by. Dont forget me. many kisses from us all to you my darling. Your A. "

*O*n a happier journey Olga, Tatiana, and Marie (above) rest by the imperial train on the way to Livadia in May 1916. (Right) Nicholas and his children sit in the sun on the roof of the greenhouse at the governor's house in Tobolsk (opposite).

TOBOLSK

After a week of travel, the family arrived in the town of Tobolsk. There they lived under guard in a large white house from August 1917 until May 1918. Although the house was cold in the winter and the food was plain, their lives were not unbearable. The girls sewed, embroidered, read, and acted in plays for the family's amusement. Alexei was allowed to play with some local boys, although sickness sometimes kept him in bed. In his diary he often wrote, "Today passed just as yesterday.... It is boring!"

In November 1917 the radical Bolshevik party led by Vladimir Ilyich Lenin seized power in St. Petersburg.

> 66 *We just came back from a walk. We built a hill out of the snow in the yard and went sliding down it…. I write so rarely because there is nothing to write. Our life here is very monotonous.* 99

—From a letter by Marie to Peter Petrov

Olga (right) chopping wood at Tobolsk. (Below) Building a snow hill in the yard. It was later destroyed by the guards, as the family could see over the fence from the top of it.

Lenin hated the tsar. New soldiers were sent to guard the Romanovs more strictly. In April 1918, a Bolshevik official arrived at the house and told Nicholas that he had come to take him from Tobolsk. Nicholas replied, "I have an ill son. I cannot leave." A few days before, Alexei had tried to slide down the stairs on his sled. He had fallen and was bleeding internally. The official insisted that Nicholas and whomever he chose to take with him would leave the next morning.

Alexandra now had to make an agonizing choice—to stay with her sick son or go with her husband. Eventually she announced her decision. "I must leave my child and share my husband's life or death." Marie was chosen to go with her parents. The other three girls would stay behind to look after Alexei. The next day at dawn, Anastasia and her sisters watched as their parents and Marie climbed into filthy horse-drawn carts and were escorted away by soldiers. Then they climbed the stairs to their room in tears.

66 *We have arranged our rooms comfortably and all four live together. We often sit in the windows looking at the people passing, and this gives us distraction...* **99** —From a letter to Anna Vyrubova

The four girls shared one room at Tobolsk (above). Anastasia's bed is on the left. Some of her favorite photographs are on the wall behind it. (Right) Alexei having tea with Olga, Tatiana, and Anastasia in Tobolsk after their parents and Marie had been taken away.

The house in Ekaterinburg was named the "House of Special Purpose" by Bolshevik officials.

EKATERINBURG

For days Anastasia and the others in Tobolsk waited anxiously for news of their parents and Marie. Then a letter arrived. Marie wrote that a train taking them to Moscow had been stopped in the Ural region. Bolshevik officials there had decided to take charge of them. Their new prison was a house in the town of Ekaterinburg. Then another letter came. In it Alexandra told the girls to "dispose of the medicines as had been agreed." "Medicines" was a code word for jewelry. If the family escaped, their jewelry would provide them with money to live on. Anastasia and her two sisters began hiding diamonds, emeralds, pearls, and rubies by sewing them into the corsets they wore under their dresses.

"I want to see you so much it's sad," Anastasia wrote to her parents and sister in Ekaterinburg. "In our thoughts, we are with you all the time." Finally, on May 23, 1918, the children were allowed to join their parents. "What great joy it was to see them and embrace them again!" Nicholas wrote in his diary on that day.

The family would live for only two months more. But for now they were together. And that was all that mattered.

> 66 *Though we know that the storm is coming nearer and nearer, our souls are at peace. Whatever happens will be through God's will.* 99

—From Alexandra's last letter to Anna Vyrubova

Epilogue

Anastasia turned seventeen on June 18, 1918. But the house behind the high fence in Ekaterinburg was no place to have a birthday celebration. All the windows had been whitewashed so that no one could look in or out. The family's food was often just black bread, tea and warmed-up leftovers from the guards' meals. They were allowed to go outside only once a day, for a walk in the garden. There, the tsar carried Alexei, who still had not recovered from his accident in Tobolsk.

Many of the guards took pleasure in humiliating the family. All of the doors to the bedrooms and even the bathroom were removed. The walls of the toilet were covered with insulting graffiti. Anastasia and her family were losing hope that they would ever escape from this terrible place. Nicholas knew that the Bolsheviks were fighting a civil war against forces loyal to him known as the Whites. If the White Army captured Ekaterinburg, they would be rescued.

After midnight on July 16, the family was awakened and told there was shooting in the town. For their own safety, they were to dress and move to the lower part of the house. Forty minutes later, Nicholas carried Alexei downstairs, followed by Alexandra, their four daughters, the family's doctor, and three of their servants. Anastasia carried her tiny pet spaniel, Jimmy. The commandant of the guards met them and led them to a small room in the cellar. "May we not sit?" Alexandra asked when she saw the room had no chairs. Two chairs were brought. Alexandra sat in one and the tsar put Alexei in the other.

The commandant returned, followed by soldiers. He read from a small piece of paper which said the family was to be executed. "What?" cried Nicholas. "What?" The commandant pulled out his pistol and shot the tsar in the head.

The room then erupted in gunfire. Alexandra was killed instantly, before she could finish making the sign of the cross. But bullets aimed at the tsar's daughters seemed to bounce off them and fly around the room. Their corsets, with the jewels sewn into them, acted like bulletproof vests. Anastasia and Marie crouched together against a wall, covering their heads with their arms. But the soldiers just continued shooting until all the moans and screams had stopped. The bodies were then wrapped in bedsheets, loaded into a truck outside, and driven off into the night.

The massacre at Ekaterinburg (left) as imagined by an artist. The cellar room (below) was photographed by White Army officers after they had dug bullets out of the walls. (Opposite) Anastasia at Tsarskoe Selo in 1916.

Eight days later, the White Army captured Ekaterinburg. In the empty house the soldiers saw bloodstains and bullet holes in the walls of the cellar room. Six months passed before more clues to the fate of the imperial family came to light. In January 1919 the remains of a huge bonfire were found near an abandoned mine shaft in a forest outside the town. The children's teachers Pierre Gilliard and Charles Gibbes were heartbroken as they helped identify many things found in the ashes—one of Alexandra's pearl earrings, the tsar's belt buckle, a piece of Alexei's cap. At the bottom of the mine shaft lay a tiny, frozen body. It was Anastasia's dog, Jimmy. The White Army investigators concluded that the Bolsheviks had killed the family and burned their bodies in the forest.

One year later, a young woman jumped from a bridge into a canal in Berlin, Germany. The police rescued her and she was taken to a hospital. One day she showed a nurse a magazine picture of the Romanovs and pointed out her resemblance to Anastasia. Later, she said that she *was* Anastasia. A guard had rescued her from the cellar room. She had come to Berlin to find relatives but in despair had jumped into the canal.

As word of her claim spread, people who had known the imperial family came to see her. Some were convinced she really was Anastasia. How else could she know so many details about the family's private life? But others were doubtful. Pierre Gilliard was one of them. Anastasia's aunt Olga, who had escaped from Russia during the civil war, hoped that the young woman might be her beloved niece. Sadly, she concluded that she was not.

For the next sixty years, the story of the woman who took the name Anna Anderson would puzzle the whole world. Could Anastasia have survived the

Alexei's spaniel, Joy (left), was found starving but alive at the house when the White Army arrived. (Above) Anna Anderson taking her own picture in the mirror in 1928 and (below) on a trip to New York in 1930. (Opposite) The bones of the imperial family and their servants were dug from this site in 1991.

horror in the cellar room? When Anna Anderson died in 1984, it seemed her identity would always be a mystery. But in 1991 some skeletons were dug out of a shallow grave in the woods near Ekaterinburg. Scientific tests determined that they were the bones of the imperial family. But the skeletons of two members of the family—thought to be Alexei and Anastasia—were missing. Could Anna Anderson have been telling

*A*unt Olga (above) escaped from Russia during the revolution and in 1945 moved to Canada. Here she is shown at her house near Toronto a year before her death in 1960. (Below) A poster for the 1956 film Anastasia, which was based on the story of Anna Anderson.

the truth? Her body had been cremated in 1984, but a piece of her intestine had been kept in a hospital where she had once had an operation. Scientists conducted tests, trying to link her blood with that of the Romanovs. They concluded that Anna Anderson could not have been Anastasia. But the bones of the real Anastasia have yet to be found. And so the mystery remains.

For more than eighty years, the diaries, letters, and photo albums of the tsar's family were kept a secret. Today we can read Anastasia's letters and see the family photographs that she collected and colored by hand. Anastasia could not know that the world depicted in the pages of her albums would soon be gone forever.

Glossary

Bolsheviks: A revolutionary political group that seized power in Russia in October of 1917. They formed the world's first communist government and ruled what became known as the Soviet Union for over seventy years.

boudoir: A woman's private sitting room.

cinematograph: An early type of silent motion picture.

commandant: A commanding officer.

corset: A tight-fitting undergarment that wraps around a woman's body and ties with laces at the back.

Cossacks: Horsemen from southern Russia who once formed part of the Russian army.

dacha: (pronounced *datcha*) The Russian word for a house or cottage used mainly for summer holidays.

Duma: The Russian parliament.

gramophone: An early type of record player.

hemophilia: A disease in which the blood does not clot properly after an injury. The result can be serious internal bleeding. It is suffered mainly by males, who inherit it from their mothers.

imperial: The tsar's family was called "imperial," rather than "royal," as he was an emperor and thus grander than a king.

Lenin: Vladimir Ilyich Lenin, a Bolshevik leader and founder of the Russian Communist Party. His older brother was hanged in 1887 for trying to assassinate Tsar Alexander III, the father of Nicholas II.

"Marie's holiday" (see page 36): This refers to the day, once a year, when a celebration is held for a particular saint. Like many Russian people, the tsar's daughters were named after saints, so they celebrated their namesake saint's day as they would a birthday.

monk: A man who is a member of a religious order and lives in a monastery. Rasputin is called a monk, but he was really a kind of wandering holy man known in Russia as a *starets*.

officer: A person who commands soldiers.

private: The lowest-ranking soldier in an army.

Queen Victoria: The queen of Great Britain from 1837 to 1901. She was also a carrier of the hemophilia gene, which her daughters then passed on to many of the royal families of Europe. Her daughter Alice married a German prince and gave birth to the future Tsarina Alexandra in 1872.

stavka: An old Russian word for an army camp, used to refer to the Russian army headquarters.

tsar (sometimes spelled **czar**): a Russian emperor. This word comes from "caesar," a Latin name for a Roman emperor.

tsarina: The wife of a tsar.

tutor: A private teacher.

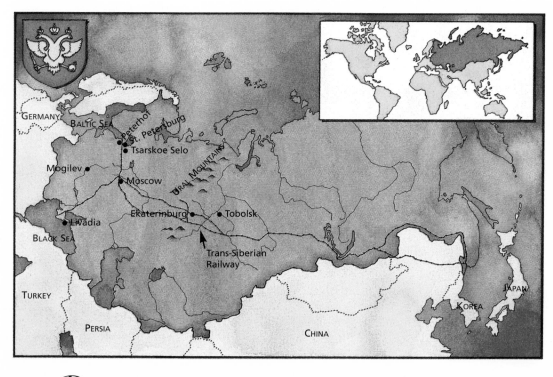

During the reign of Nicholas II, the Russian empire covered one-sixth of the globe.

Picture Credits

Every effort has been made to correctly attribute all material reproduced in this book. If any errors have unwittingly occurred, we will be happy to correct them in future editions.

The endpapers of this book and all black-and-white and hand-colored photographs, album pages and quotes from the letters of the Grand Duchess Anastasia Nicholaievna, unless otherwise designated, are courtesy of the **State Archive of the Russian Federation, Moscow.**

All color photographs, unless otherwise designated, are **by Peter Christopher** © 1996.

Front cover: Photo of cover by Clive Champion; Portrait enhancement by Ted Smith

Brown Brothers: front cover portrait; back cover (all); 3 (inset); 11; 14 (top and bottom left); 21 (right); 56-57

Beinecke Rare Book and Manuscript Library, Yale University Library: 18 (top); 22; 27 (right); 31 (left); 36 (top and right); 41 (black and white photos only)

Bibliothèque cantonale et universitaire, Lausanne, Fonds Gilliard, IS 1916: 16 (bottom left and right); 27 (left); 49 (top); 50 (bottom); 51; 53; 58; 59 (right)

The Broadlands Archive: 8 (left); 23 (bottom)

Byington Collection: 62 (top)

Forbes Magazine Collection, New York: 10 (bottom right), photo by Larry Stein; 12, photo by Joseph Coscia Jr.

Hulton-Deutsch: 10 (left); 52 (right)

Mary Evans Picture Library: 13 (left); 59 (left)

Jack McMaster: 63

The Pavlosk Museum: 15 (bottom right), photo by Peter Christopher

Peter Kurth Collection: 60 (top and bottom right)

RIA-Novosti/Sovfoto: 9 (top)

State Archive of Film and Photographic Documents, St. Petersburg: 13 (right)

The State Hermitage Museum: 8 (right); 9 (bottom), both photos by PC

Virginia Museum of Fine Arts, Richmond, VA. Bequest of Lillian Thomas Pratt. Photo: Katherine Wetzel, © 1996: I

Werhner Collection, The Luton Hoo Foundation: 30 (right); 54 (all); 55 (all); 60 (left)

Woronzow-Daschkow, Hilarion Graf Collection, Hoover Institution Archive, Stanford University: 10 (top right)

Acknowledgments

Madison Press Books would like to extend special thanks to: Lyubov Tyutunnik, Sergei Mironenko and Aliya Barkovets of the State Archive of the Russian Federation, Moscow; Kate Murdoch of Taylor and Murdoch Bookbinders; Paul Byington; The Trustees of the Broadlands Archives; Kathryn Dean; Katya Kazakina; Robert Kenner; Peter Kurth; Maia Nosenkis; Howell Perkins of the Virginia Museum of Fine Arts; Igor Sarkissov; Enver Shidaev; Catherine Thomas of The Forbes Collection; Tanya Yermolayeva

Credits

Design and Art Direction:
Gordon Sibley Design

Editorial Director: Hugh M. Brewster

Project Editor: Mireille Majoor

Text Editor: Shelley Tanaka

Research and Translation: Alla Savranskaia

Color Photography: Peter Christopher

Map: Jack McMaster

Production Director: Susan Barrable

Production Co-ordinator: Donna Chong

Color Separation: Colour Technologies

Printing and Binding:
Butler & Tanner Limited

ANASTASIA'S ALBUM was produced by Madison Press Books, which is under the direction of Albert E. Cummings

Primary Works and Sources Consulted

Bokhanov, Alexander, Manfred Knodt, Vladimir Oustimenko, Zinaida Peregudova, and Lyubov Tyutunnik. *The Romanovs: Love, Power and Tragedy.* Italy: Keppi Productions, 1993.

Botkin, Gleb. *The Real Romanovs.* New York: Fleming H. Revell, 1931.

Dehn, Lili. *The Real Tsaritsa.* Boston: Little, Brown, 1922.

Gilliard, Pierre. *Thirteen Years at the Russian Court.* London: Hutchinson & Co., 1921.

King, Greg. *The Last Empress: The Life and Times of Alexandra Feodorovna, Tsarina of Russia.* New York: Birch Lane Press, 1994.

Kurth, Peter. *Anastasia: The Riddle of Anna Anderson.* Boston: Little, Brown, 1983.

Kurth, Peter. *Tsar: The Lost World of Nicholas and Alexandra.* New York, Toronto, London: Little, Brown, 1995.

Lyons, Marvin. *Nicholas II: The Last Tsar.* New York: St. Martin's Press, 1974.

Massie, Robert K. *Nicholas and Alexandra.* New York: Atheneum, 1967.

Massie, Robert K. *The Romanov Family Album.* New York: The Vendome Press, 1982.

Michael, Prince of Greece. *Nicholas and Alexandra: The Family Albums.* London: Tauris Parke Books, 1992.

Radzinsky, Edvard. *The Last Tsar.* New York: Doubleday, 1992.

Trewin, John. *The House of Special Purpose.* New York: Stein & Day, 1975.

Viroubova, Anna. *Memories of the Russian Court.* New York: Macmillan, 1923.

Vorres, Ian. *The Last Grand-Duchess.* London: Hutchinson & Co., 1964.